BILL GATES

JEANNE M. LESINSKI

In Consultation with Martha Cosgrove,
M.A. and Reading Specialist

JUST THE FACTS BIOGRAPHIES

LERNER PUBLICATIONS COMPANY / MINNEAPOLIS

To my mother, who bought me my first computer

Martha Cosgrove has a master's degree from the University of Minnesota in secondary education, with an emphasis on developmental and remedial reading. She is licensed in 7–12 English and language arts, developmental reading, and remedial reading. She has had several works published, and she gives numerous state and national presentations in her areas of expertise.

Lerner Publications Company
A division of Lerner Publishing Group
241 First Avenue North
Minneapolis, MN 55401 U.S.A.

Website address: www.lernerbooks.com

Library of Congress Cataloging-in-Publication Data

Lesinski, Jeanne M.
   Bill Gates / by Jeanne M. Lesinski.
      p.   cm. — (Just the facts biographies)
   Includes bibliographical references and index.
   ISBN-13: 978–0–8225–2642–1 (lib. bdg. : alk. paper)
   ISBN-10: 0–8225–2642–5 (lib. bdg. : alk. paper)
   1. Gates, Bill, 1955– –Juvenile literature. 2. Businessmen–United States–Biography–Juvenile literature. 3. Computer software industry–United States–History–Juvenile literature. 4. Microsoft Corporation–History–Juvenile literature. I. Title. II. Series.
   HD9696.63.U62G3745   2006
   338.7'610053'092–dc22   2005008294

Manufactured in the United States of America
1 2 3 4 5 6 – BP – 11 10 09 08 07 06

CONTENTS

CHAPTER 1

GROWING UP

BILL GATES is a famous billionaire. People all over the world know who he is. He is the man who started and runs Microsoft Corporation, the world's biggest computer software company. He fell in love with computers when he was thirteen. He still loves working in the computer business. But people may not see this Bill Gates. They only see the billionaire.

Bill has sometimes joked about having the name of his father—William Henry Gates. He says that his parents would have given him a more unusual name if they had known he would become famous. A one-of-a-kind name would be more fitting for such a one-of-a-kind person. But how could the Gateses have known this about their small and shy son? How could they have known that he would one day build a company of more than thirty thousand workers? How could they have known that he would be the leader of great changes in technology? How could they have known that he would become the richest man in the world?

EARLY DAYS

Bill Gates's father, William Gates II, served in the U.S. Army in World War II (1939–1945). Afterward, he studied law at the University of Washington in Seattle, Washington. There, he fell in love with Mary Maxwell. She was charming and full of energy. The two married in 1951 and settled in Seattle. William, who went by the name Bill, joined a law firm in Seattle. Mary taught school.

The couple's first child was born in 1953, a daughter named Kristianne. Two years later, on October 28, 1955, William Henry "Little Bill" Gates III joined the family. His younger sister, Libby, was born in 1964.

Right away, Little Bill showed good humor and high energy, rocking in his cradle. Later, he grew to love a rocking horse. He rode it for hours. Little Bill discovered that rocking improved his ability to think.

IT'S A FACT!

Bill has rocked back and forth since he was a tiny child. His mother believed it helped calm him. Bill believes it helps him concentrate.

At school, Bill was the youngest student in his class. He was small for his age and somewhat clumsy. But he did very well in schoolwork. Certain subjects, such as math and science, were easy for him. Bill read a lot too. He read whole textbooks. He entered and won reading contests at the local library. At the age of eight, Bill started to read *The World Book Encyclopedia.* "I was determined to read straight through every volume," he recalled. He read up to the letter P. Then he got interested in other activities.

Mary Gates was smart and full of energy. She volunteered with organizations in her community and was very busy. So her mother, Adelle Maxwell, cared for the grandchildren after school. Adelle's nickname was Gam. Gam had snacks and activities for Bill and his sisters after school.

Little Bill's parents did not allow their children to watch television during the week. The family read and played games often. Board games, puzzles, and card games went on for hours. Gam loved card games. She taught the children to play bridge. She nicknamed Bill "Trey," after the card player's term for "three" and because he was William Henry Gates III.

After dinner on Sundays, the entire family would play games. "The play was quite serious. Winning mattered," Bill's father recalled. Trey didn't like to lose.

IT'S A FACT!

Bill's mother used the game Hangman to let Bill and his older sister Kristianne know that the Gates family would be growing to include another baby. The hangman message was "A Little Visitor Is Coming Soon."

LOOKING FOR A CHALLENGE

When Bill was in fourth grade, the family moved to a new home in Seattle. By this time, Bill was bored with school. He worked hard in the subjects he liked, math and reading. But he made little effort in subjects he found boring. Bill was left-handed. But he sometimes took notes with his right hand. He did this just to give himself a little challenge when bored in class.

At the school library, Bill helped to find misshelved and lost books. In the library, Bill discovered the work of Leonardo da Vinci. Da Vinci was a scientist and artist who lived in Italy from 1452 to 1519. He studied and drew the human body. He sketched flying machines. Bill decided that he wanted to be a scientist too.

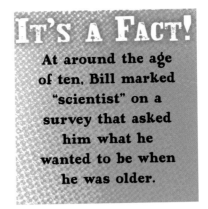

IT'S A FACT!

At around the age of ten, Bill marked "scientist" on a survey that asked him what he wanted to be when he was older.

Bill was not interested in team sports. He tried Little League baseball, but it was too slow for him. Roller-skating, tennis, and skiing were more exciting. In summer, he swam, dove, and sailed on

Lake Washington in Seattle. The family rented cabins on the Hood Canal near Puget Sound, a large ocean inlet in the northwest corner of Washington. There, they gathered with friends for picnics, games, and campfires. Bill also joined a Boy Scout troop. The troop took hiking and camping trips, which fed Bill's craving for adventure.

FINDING A FOCUS

In sixth grade, Bill still wasn't very focused. "My desk was always messy, and I didn't seem to be paying attention. I was always out there on the playground trying to form some sort of group of guys, or sort of laughing about something when you weren't supposed to be laughing," he remembered later. Bill did like one school group, the Century Club. It was made up of smart sixth graders. With the Century Club, Bill went on educational field trips. They also played board games and talked about books and current events.

But he did do well in a special economics class at school. For this class, he made up a pretend business report called "Invest with Gatesway Incorporated." Bill imagined himself as a young inventor who made and sold a new product.

Bill and Mary Gates became worried about Bill when he was ready for junior high. "He was so small and shy, in need of protection, and his interests were so very different from the typical sixth grader's," his father remembered. The Gateses talked about sending their son to a private school. There, classes would be smaller. Rules would be stricter. They wanted Bill to learn good study habits. They wanted him to get ready for college and a career. Finally, they decided to send Bill to Lakeside School. Lakeside was a private school in Seattle for boys in grades seven through twelve. There, students wore jackets and neckties. They carried briefcases and had assigned seating–even at lunch.

As an eighth grader, Bill (left) was smaller than many of his classmates.

Bill started school at Lakeside in 1967. He tried to get used to his new school and schoolmates. But he still didn't work hard at his classes. He was a B student, except in honors algebra. In that, he earned an A minus. He hung out with other students interested in math and science. As usual, he read a lot. Favorite books included biographies. He read about the French emperor Napoleon Bonaparte (1769–1821) and U.S. president Franklin D. Roosevelt (1882–1945).

Bill and the other students discovered a new machine at their school in 1968. It was a fascinating machine called a Teletype machine. This machine had a keyboard, a printer, and a paper-tape punch and reader. It could be hooked up to a telephone by placing the receiver in a special cradle. The Teletype machine could send and receive information through the telephone lines.

At this time, personal computers had not yet been invented. Instead, businesses and universities used mainframe computers. Mainframes were bigger than refrigerators. Holes punched in paper tapes instructed the computers to perform tasks. Researchers at universities and laboratories used the computers to analyze data (large amounts of information). Businesses used mainframes to figure out monthly bills for customers.

Mainframe computers cost millions of dollars. So businesses and universities often shared a single computer. Users at different places made paper tapes carrying instructions. Then they sent the instructions to the mainframe they shared. To do that, they used Teletype machines and telephone lines.

THE TELETYPE

In 1844, the inventor Samuel F. B. Morse created the telegraph. The telegraph sent information across great distances through a wire and was extremely helpful. One problem with the design was that operators had to be at each end of the wire to send and receive the information. Many people thought it would be a good idea to create a device that would type the incoming messages and allow messages to be sent without someone waiting to write them down. This idea for a new machine eventually became the Teletype.

The first few designs of the Teletype were very complicated. The machines were connected to one another through telegraph lines. They had to be linked perfectly to send messages correctly. By the 1910s, the first successful Teletypes were being used. Within the next twenty years, Teletypes became an important communication tool. But by the 1970s, when Bill and his friends at Lakeside began working with Teletypes, they were becoming old technology.

Bill looks on as Paul Allen—an older Lakeside student—types at the keyboard of the ASR-33 Teletype machine in 1968.

MASTERING THE COMPUTER

At first, the Lakeside students did not know a thing about computers. Their teachers didn't know much more. But they began to figure them out. The user wrote instructions, called programs. Then the computer gave answers to problems and questions. If a program wasn't written right, the computer wouldn't come up with useful answers.

Bill was excited to master the computer. "I wrote my first . . . program when I was thirteen years old," he recalled. "It was for playing tic-tac-toe." The computer was huge and slow. But Bill couldn't stop thinking about it. Bill had found his focus.

Lakeside had no classes in computing. So teachers and students taught themselves from computer manuals. Bill and other students spent as much time as they could using the computer. They learned different programming languages. One language was BASIC–Beginner's All-purpose Symbolic Instruction Code. Another was FORTRAN, a programming language used by scientists. Each language had its own rules and vocabulary.

The students wrote simple programs, or software. The programs grew in size and complexity. Bill wrote a program to play the game Risk using a computer. In this game, players pretend to take over the world. Another student wrote a program to calculate grade point averages.

Bill worked in the school's computer room a lot. Some students complained that he was hogging the equipment. These same students often came to Bill for answers when they got stuck with programming problems.

In ninth grade, Bill started doing better in school. "I hadn't been getting good grades," he explained, "but I decided to get all A's without taking a book home. I didn't go to math class, because I knew enough and had read ahead, and I placed within the top ten people in the nation on an aptitude exam. That established my independence and taught me I didn't need to rebel anymore." Bill became a straight-A student.

PAYING THE BILLS

General Electric charged the Lakeside students eighty-nine dollars per month for the Teletype. They also charged eight dollars an hour for computer time. The computer students quickly racked up big bills. The Lakeside Mothers' Club helped pay for these bills through a yearly garage sale. But the students needed to find other ways to pay for computer time.

Bill's parents paid his school tuition and bought his books. But they insisted he pay for his own computer fees. "This is what drove me to the commercial side of the software business," Bill explained. He wanted to work with computers and get paid for it.

A big influence on Bill was his best friend, Kent Evans. Kent was very interested in computers and in the business world. And he showed confidence that was unusual for someone his age. For a time, he and Bill were inseparable. "We read *Fortune* [business magazine] together; we were going to conquer the world," Bill said.

WORKING COMPUTER JOBS

The Lakeside computer students were very happy when the Computer Center Corporation (later nicknamed C-Cubed) opened in Seattle. The company owned a mainframe computer. The Lakeside students hooked up to it using a Teletype machine and phone lines. Few people understood computers in those years. So the company director relied on the Lakeside students for help.

The students worked at night when the company was closed for the day. They tested the computer and fixed bugs (flaws) in the programs. Students took city buses from Lakeside to go to C-Cubed. They stayed there for hours. Sometimes Bill snuck out of his bedroom at night to go work on the computer. If he missed the last bus, he'd have to walk three miles to get home.

CRASHING ON PURPOSE

The students of Lakeside were allowed free access to the C-Cubed computer. The company told them to find ways to crash the system. The company hoped to learn from each crash and improve its system.

Bill, Paul Allen, and others found a way to break into the accounting system at C-Cubed. They got passwords and changed how much computer-use time they were being billed for. The company found out about their experiment and developed a new security system. The company asked the students to break it. It took the students only a half hour. Even so, the company fined the students for changing their bills and banned the students from using the system for an entire summer.

Eventually, C-Cubed went out of business. Then Bill and other students found weekend and summer jobs writing programs for other computer companies. Computer programs are written in steps. The first step is to develop the process for solving a problem. The next step is to write "code"–a program that will solve the problem. Gates and an older student named Paul Allen wrote computer code in return for free computer time. They also got paid.

One company laid hoses across highways. The hoses collected data about traffic patterns. The company hired Bill to count the data and put it into a computer. He hired several Lakeside students to help count, while he input the data by punched tape. Then he printed out the results.

During Bill's junior (third) year, Lakeside merged with another school. Saint Nicholas was an all-girls' school. The merged school had five hundred more students. This made the class schedules hard to figure out by hand. Each student went to eight classes a day. Some classes met only one day a week. Some classes included an extra two-hour laboratory period.

Some teachers tried to write a computer program to create a schedule. But they couldn't do it on their own. They asked Bill and his friend Kent Evans for help. The two boys spent long hours at the task. They often went without sleep. As the deadline neared, tragedy struck. Kent fell to his death in a mountain climbing accident.

Bill was devastated. "I had never thought of people dying," he remembers. He was supposed to speak at Kent's memorial service. But he was too upset to do so. "For two weeks I couldn't do anything at all," Bill wrote. After some time, Bill continued to work on the scheduling program. He and Paul Allen finally finished it.

During Bill's senior (fourth) year, he got a new job. He was a programmer for a company called TRW, Inc. So was Paul, who had already graduated. The company was writing a computer program to control an electricity grid. Bill's school let him miss classes so he could attend work. The job was considered his senior project.

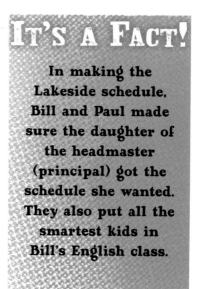

IT'S A FACT!

In making the Lakeside schedule, Bill and Paul made sure the daughter of the headmaster (principal) got the schedule she wanted. They also put all the smartest kids in Bill's English class.

AN IMPORTANT FRIENDSHIP

Bill and Paul also tried to build their own computer and software. Computer chips are the brains of a computer. When Bill was in high school, computer chips were still very simple. So Bill and Paul tried to think of a simple job for their machine. They came up with Traf-O-Data. This system counted and analyzed traffic patterns.

The two young men never finished the project. But their friendship grew as they worked together. "I was lucky in my early teens to become friends with Paul Allen," Bill once remarked. "Paul had lots of answers to things I was curious about. . . . I was more of a math person than Paul, and I understood software better than anyone he knew. . . . We liked to challenge each other."

Bill was also interested in things besides computing. In the summer of 1972, he worked as a page (a person who delivers messages, gives tours, and does other jobs) in the U.S. Congress in Washington, D.C. By this time, Bill the shy young man had grown confident. He had starred in three school plays. He played chess and a Chinese game called Go. He drove his family's red Mustang convertible. He water-skied and went to the senior prom.

Bill had lots of options after high school. He had good grades and test scores. He did well on a college test called the Scholastic Aptitude Test

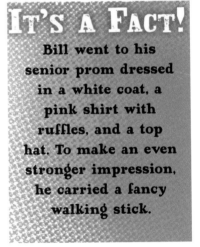

IT'S A FACT!

Bill went to his senior prom dressed in a white coat, a pink shirt with ruffles, and a top hat. To make an even stronger impression, he carried a fancy walking stick.

(SAT). He scored 800 (a perfect score) on the math portion and 700 on the verbal portion. He won a National Merit Scholarship. This award of money for college is given to students based on their test scores, their school and after-school activities, their personality, and other information. Bill toured several colleges in the eastern United States and applied to Harvard (in Massachusetts), Yale (in Connecticut), and Princeton (in New Jersey). Bill was accepted at all three of those top U.S. universities. He chose to attend Harvard.

2

SPREADING HIS WINGS

IN 1973, WHEN HE WAS ALMOST eighteen, Bill Gates began his studies at Harvard University. Harvard is in Cambridge, near Boston. During his freshman year, he studied several subjects. He took classes in advanced math, Greek literature, English, social science, and organic chemistry. He often skipped his own classes and attended other classes just for fun. He used the university's computers and continued working on his Traf-O-Data project.

At hamburger restaurants, Bill discovered the video game Pong and played it often. With other math students, he had serious talks about many subjects. Bill believed that one day average people would own their own computers. The other students laughed at the idea. They couldn't imagine computers smaller than the mainframes at the university's computer center.

At Harvard, Bill was no longer the smartest student in math class. Bill had planned to major in math. Now, he thought about majoring in law or one of the sciences. He also thought about taking time off from college and getting a job. He interviewed with several companies.

During his sophomore year, Bill met a math and science student named Steve Ballmer. Ballmer lived in the same dormitory (residence hall) at Harvard as Bill did. Steve was outgoing and charming. He made sure Bill had a life outside of his studies. The friends played the video game Breakout and attended all-night poker games. "He'd play poker until six in the morning, then I'd run into him at breakfast and discuss applied mathematics," Ballmer recalled. Together, Gates and Ballmer took graduate-level courses in math and economics (the study of money and business in society).

WRITING SOFTWARE PROGRAMS

Meanwhile, Paul Allen had accepted a job near Boston. He and Bill stayed close friends. They realized that their traffic-analyzing machine was not going to get sold. So they decided to focus on creating useful software. They talked for many hours about possible software projects. They also kept up on the computer industry's latest changes.

In 1975, the Altair 8800 became the first personal computer to be sold to the public. The computer didn't look like much. And the buyer had to put it together from a kit. Only people who were very interested in electronics bought this early computer. The Altair 8800 may have been simple. But it was still a computer, and it needed software. Gates and Allen decided to write a program for the Altair. Their program would allow the machine to run other programs such as BASIC. They hoped to sell the program to the

IT'S A FACT!

The Altair looked like a box with several rows of little lights. It had several more rows of tiny switches across the front. It had no keyboard or disk drive.

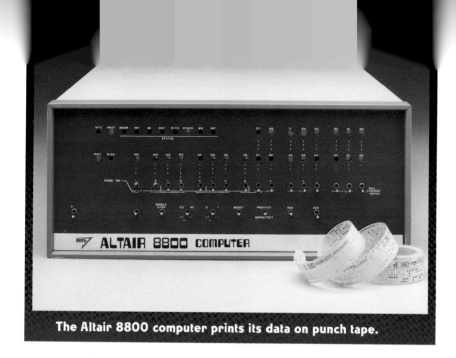

The Altair 8800 computer prints its data on punch tape.

Altair's manufacturer, Micro Instrumentation and Telemetry System (MITS).

For six weeks, Bill almost lived at the Harvard computer center. Sometimes he napped in a corner of the computer lab or slumped over a keyboard. Allen came to the center when he was off work. Gates and Allen hired several other Harvard students to write small parts of their BASIC program. They called the program MS-BASIC. Ed Roberts, the creator of the Altair, agreed to buy the rights to use MS-BASIC in his computers. Afterward, Gates and Allen still had to fix dozens of bugs in the program.

In the spring of 1975, Bill finished his classes at Harvard. He wasn't sure if he should return in

the fall. Paul Allen had accepted a job with MITS
as its director of software. Bill realized that he was
standing at an important point in history.
Technology was about to change in a big way.

FOUNDING MICROSOFT

For years, people had used adding machines to
figure out large sums. They had typed documents,
including whole books, page by page on
typewriters. If a typist needed more than one copy
of a document, he or she placed carbon paper
between sheets of typing paper. The carbon
transferred type from the top sheet of paper to the
sheets behind it. Making changes and correcting
errors took a long time. It was also expensive.

Bill saw that a personal computer would make
these and other tasks much easier. He wanted to
help solve millions of people's everyday problems.
And he wanted to make money in the process.

He decided to leave Harvard to start a
software company with Paul Allen. Bill's parents
did not agree with his decision. They tried to talk
him out of it. So Bill went back to Harvard for a
semester or two. But in the end, his software
business won out.

In 1977, when Bill was twenty-two, he left
Harvard for Albuquerque, New Mexico. Paul
Allen had quit MITS in 1976. To start a software
business together, he and Bill registered the name
Microsoft with the state of New Mexico. They
were in business.

But could their business work when there were
so many hackers? Back then, computer hackers
were people who would give away their own

Microsoft had its first offices in this Albuquerque, New
Mexico, office building from September 1976 to
December 1978.

programs for free. And they would copy other people's programs. Bill caused a stir in 1975 when he wrote a letter in the *Computer Notes* newsletter. He said that computer users were stealing if they copied computer programs. Instead, users should buy them. Bill argued that software programs were "intellectual property." That means they should be legally protected through copyright, like books are. Then the programs would be protected by law from people using them for free. Because of Bill's efforts, copying computer programs became illegal.

IT'S A FACT!

Bill quickly saw that most people who were using the BASIC program hadn't bothered to buy the software. They were simply copying it. One estimate said only 10 percent of users owned the software legally.

Soon companies like Apple, Commodore, and Radio Shack got into the personal computer business. Computer makers developed more powerful chips. As a result, software programs became more powerful too. The new programs could perform more complicated tasks. Word-processing programs, for example, allowed users to easily move around words and paragraphs within typed documents. The programs also allowed users to choose different styles and sizes of type. Other programs could show, move, and change graphic images (illustrations and photos, for example). And the programs could perform all of these tasks faster than ever before.

A COMPUTER ON EVERY DESK

Years earlier, Gates and Allen had sold the rights to MS-BASIC to MITS. But the two men needed the rights back for their company. MITS agreed to give

Bill Gates *(left)* **and Paul Allen** *(right)* **worked together writing computer programs.**

the rights back to Gates and Allen. At Microsoft, they wrote BASIC programs for the various new computers on the market. Each brand of computer was slightly different from the others. So each needed its own version of the BASIC program.

Microsoft sold its BASIC program for a very low price. Bill believed that the company would make a profit even with the low price. That's because so many people would buy the program. Microsoft's motto was "a computer on every desk and in every home."

Bill poses in front of some computers that were available in the early 1980s.

Bill could probably have gotten money from his family to help start his business. But he didn't want to. He wanted Microsoft to support itself from the start. For three years, he worked long hours. Sometimes he worked sixteen hours a day. He wrote computer code. He also handled the business end of the company. He made sales calls to companies like General Electric, National Cash Register, and Citibank. These big companies needed software for their mainframes and other computers. He also talked with computer makers about selling MS-BASIC and other programming languages with their machines.

Bill was now in his early twenties. But his slight build, messy hair, and freckles made him look like a teenager. His youthful looks sometimes made possible buyers nervous. But then they heard him talk about his company's products. They could tell that he knew the business. As Microsoft sold more programs, Bill hired more employees. Many were old friends from Lakeside School.

For employees, Microsoft was more like a college than a business. There was no dress code telling employees what to wear. In fact, many programmers wore jeans. They hung posters on the walls and listened to rock music if they wanted. The company gave out free sodas. Work hours were very flexible. Some programmers arrived in the afternoon and worked until evening. Then they grabbed a bite to eat, maybe went to a movie, and came back to work late at night. They straggled home in the early morning hours. Then they returned to work again around noon.

Although work at Microsoft was relaxed, the programmers were serious. They were going to change the world. But exactly how much—and in what ways—wasn't clear yet.

No one at Microsoft worked harder than Bill Gates. He worked so hard that he often forgot to take care of his appearance or to eat meals. Sometimes, when his secretary came to work in the morning, she found her boss asleep on the floor of his office. Bill did find time to relax. He went to movies. He bought a used sports car and took high-speed nighttime drives. He got many speeding tickets.

It's a Fact!

Bill often sped around in Paul Allen's new Chevy Monza. On one outing, he rounded a curve too quickly and drove the new car into a barbed-wire fence.

The Albuquerque, New Mexico, police took this photograph of Bill in 1977 after a traffic violation.

At least once, Paul Allen had to bail him out of jail when Bill forgot his driver's license.

Microsoft no longer had ties to MITS. And it was often hard to convince programmers to move to Albuquerque. It was far from most major universities and big cities. So, in 1978, Bill decided to move the company. By then it had twelve employees. Most computer companies were located in California. But Gates's ties to his family were strong. He decided to move Microsoft to Bellevue, Washington, near Seattle.

Bill wanted Microsoft to be very successful. He believed that personal computers would become very important for businesses. He felt sure that many people would want a computer at home. To prepare for this, Microsoft needed to sell more than just language products like BASIC. It needed to sell word-processing and other kinds of software.

Bill also saw that Microsoft needed smarter, more efficient business practices. Bill knew that his college friend Steve Ballmer would be very helpful, even though he knew little about computers. Ballmer had business experience and social skills. As it turned out, Ballmer was available. He became Bill's assistant and one of the company's best promoters.

DEALING WITH IBM

In 1980, a company called International Business Machines (IBM) was the leading maker of mainframe computers. That year, IBM decided to start making personal computers too. IBM bosses wanted a product ready for sale in a short time. So they decided not to build their own computer from scratch. Instead, they built one using parts that were already made by other companies. And they didn't write their own software for the IBM personal computer (PC), either. For that, they contacted Microsoft.

Bill Gates agreed to provide IBM with a group of software programs. One program was a disk operating system. The operating system, or OS, is the master program that runs the computer. It controls the keyboard, the monitor, and the system that stores information.

For a year, nearly half of the sixty employees at Microsoft worked day and night on the IBM project. They gave their OS the name MS-DOS. Bill licensed the system to IBM on a royalty basis. That meant IBM would pay a royalty (a percentage of the money) to Microsoft for each copy of MS-DOS that IBM sold. IBM introduced its personal computer in 1981. Buyers snapped it up. Royalties began to pour into Microsoft.

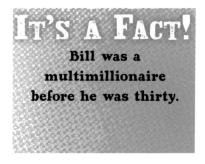

IT'S A FACT!

Bill was a multimillionaire before he was thirty.

Other computer makers built computers similar to IBM's. These computers came to be called clones. The clones needed software too. Bill was right there, offering MS-DOS and other products for the clones. Royalties began to come in from PC makers everywhere. MS-DOS became the standard OS for IBM PCs and clones. Nearly all the computer users who were using MS-DOS could share files and documents.

By the end of 1982, Microsoft had sold $32 million in software. The company had about two hundred employees. But it soon lost a very important person. Paul Allen learned that he had Hodgkin's disease, a treatable form of cancer. He left Microsoft in early 1983 to focus on other goals. Bill was sorry to see his friend leave. But he had a company to run. Microsoft depended on him for leadership. He had to decide what products to make and how to sell them. He knew a lot more was going to happen in the computer industry.

APPLE VS. MICROSOFT

One of the most important U.S. computer companies at this time was Apple. Steve Wozniak and Steve Jobs had started the company in 1975. They released the Apple 1 computer in 1976. To make its computers easy to use, Apple Computers introduced a system called the graphical user interface, or GUI (pronounced "GOO-ee"). The GUI system involved a device called a mouse. Apple users used the mouse to point at small pictures on the screen to control their computers. They didn't have to remember complicated word and number commands like a user did with MS-DOS.

Bill Gates was watching what Apple Computers was doing. He could see that making computers easier to use was an important step. He believed that GUI was the key.

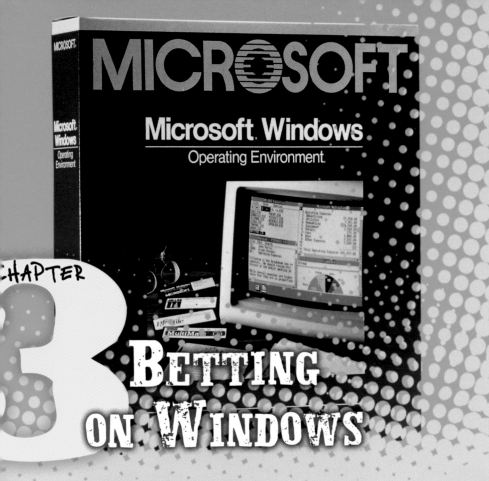

CHAPTER

3

BETTING ON WINDOWS

DURING THE 1980s, Microsoft grew
quickly. In 1982, the company introduced a
spreadsheet program called Multiplan. The
program helped business people do accounting
and other financial work. The next year,
Microsoft came out with Word. Word was a
word-processing program featuring WYSIWYG
(pronounced "wizzy-wig"). That stands for

(Above)
**Microsoft
Windows 1.0
was
launched in
November
1983.**

"What You See Is What You Get." WYSIWYG showed words on the screen exactly as they would appear on paper, whether printed in italics, boldface, or another type style.

At that time, Microsoft mostly made software. But Bill wanted to make one piece of hardware. He wanted a mouse that could be used with an upcoming GUI program. He also formed Microsoft Press, which published books about how to use Microsoft programs. He opened offices or licensed other companies to sell Microsoft products in Japan, Europe, and Australia.

Microsoft continued its relationship with IBM. It licensed MS-DOS for IBM's new, powerful IBM PC-AT. Programmers at the two companies worked together on a more advanced operating system, OS/2. But each team had a different idea of what the product should be. In the end, IBM finished OS/2 by itself. IBM left out many ideas that Microsoft had brought to the project.

WORKING ON WINDOWS

Instead of OS/2, Bill Gates created an operating system he called Windows. Windows was named for the separate frames users could create on the computer screen. And Windows would use GUI. Instead of memorizing commands, users would operate the computer with a mouse. They would point and click on small pictures called icons. Windows would be user-friendly. It would let people run more than one program at a time. And it would let them easily move information from one program to another.

Bill bet the future of his company on Windows. He had big plans for the new OS. He spent hours thinking about it. What would it look like? How would it work? Should the windows overlap or appear next to each other? What should the icons look like? What colors should borders and titles be?

Thirty programmers worked on the first version of Windows. They loved the challenge of creating an exciting new product. They often worked very long hours to meet deadlines. By 1984, Windows was way behind schedule. Bill wanted to make sure that Windows was a high-quality program. Sometimes he asked programmers to throw out weeks' worth of computer code and start over. At some point, Bill decided that enough was enough. He'd have to finish the first version of Windows and make improvements later.

Like the programmers, Bill had a hectic work schedule. Along with Steve Ballmer, he was the head salesperson for Microsoft products. And he liked to know—and have his say—about what was going on in all areas of Microsoft.

Bill didn't have much time for life outside of work. But by this time, he owned a house in his parents' neighborhood. The house had an indoor swimming pool but little furniture. The den contained a desk and computer. The room was cluttered with computer magazines. An e-mail system allowed Microsoft employees to send messages to each other's computers at work. Bill's home computer was tied into the system through phone lines. He could—and did—send messages to his employees from

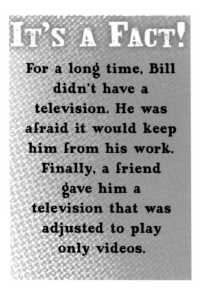

IT'S A FACT!

For a long time, Bill didn't have a television. He was afraid it would keep him from his work. Finally, a friend gave him a television that was adjusted to play only videos.

home, sometimes in the middle of the night.
Despite all the work, Bill made a point to see his
family often. He sometimes had friends over for
parties or to swim in his indoor pool.

DATING LIFE

As male coworkers got married, Bill threw
bachelor parties. He himself had several
girlfriends. For a year, he dated Jill Bennett. She
worked for another computer company. Bill and
Jill shared an interest in computers and tennis.
And they had some friends in common. What
they didn't have enough of, though, was time.
Bill was at the office more than he was at home.
Dating took too much of his time and energy.

Another girlfriend was Ann Winblad. Bill
and Ann met at a computer show in 1984. They
dated for three years.
They studied together
and went on vacations.
They went to South
America and Africa. Ann
was several years older
than Bill. She was also
ready to settle down. But

IT'S A FACT!

Ann Winblad even
talked Bill into
giving up his favorite
food—cheeseburgers—
for a time.

**Ann Winblad, also
a software engineer,
dated Bill for three
years beginning
in 1984.**

Bill wasn't ready for marriage. After he and Ann
stopped dating, they remained friends.

In 1985, Bill celebrated his thirtieth birthday.
He had a roller-skating party for family, friends,
and coworkers. This year also marked the tenth
anniversary of Microsoft. For ten years, Bill had
focused hard on his business. All his work was
paying off. In 1985, the company sold $140

million worth of products, including operating systems, business software, hardware, and how-to books.

Even better, the first version of Windows had been sold in the United States that year. Windows had a few bugs. And other computer companies hadn't yet written many programs to run with it. Some computer specialists wondered if Windows was really the future of personal computing. But for Bill Gates, Windows was only the beginning.

He had never imagined that his company would grow so big so fast. In fact, he had wanted to keep the staff at about one thousand employees. Yet Microsoft continued to grow. MS-DOS was bringing in steady income. Bill no longer knew the names of all his employees.

In 1986, Microsoft moved its headquarters. The new location was just outside of Redmond, Washington. The headquarters had four X-shaped buildings and was located in a park. In the middle of these buildings was an artificial lake. The lake soon became known as "Lake Bill." Every employee had an office with a computer. Everyone had a high-quality, comfortable chair and a nice view of the outdoors. They could get free beverages. Candy and other snacks were available at a low cost. If the weather was nice, workers grabbed food from the cafeteria and found spots on the lawn to eat their lunch. There, people played musical instruments, juggled, and rode unicycles. They played basketball, soccer, and softball.

The company grew to more than twenty thousand employees. Microsoft constructed more

Microsoft's offices are located in Redmond, Washington.

buildings. Yet one thing remained basically the
same—the flat corporate structure. "Flat" meant
that the company had just a few managers to
keep the employees moving along at their jobs.
With e-mail, workers could quickly send memos
and notes to many people at once, so the
company needed few secretaries. Staff could and
did e-mail Bill directly with their ideas, questions,
and gripes.

MAKING MILLIONAIRES

During Microsoft's first ten years, Bill gave many
employees stock options, or shares of the company.
If you own stock, you own part of a company. As
long as Microsoft was privately owned, employees
could not sell their shares. In 1986, Microsoft "went
public." That meant Microsoft stopped being
privately owned. The company allowed outsiders to
buy stock shares in the company. The company
sold shares on the stock exchange (the system that
buys and sells stock worldwide). Institutions and
people who were not employees of Microsoft could
buy them. As a publicly owned company, Microsoft
could sell stock at whatever price people were
willing to pay.

Some businesses sell shares of stock to make money so they can grow. But Microsoft did not need to make money that way. It had no debt. It made a profit of $30 million during the first six months of 1985. Yet Bill did need to keep his hardworking employees happy. The morning that Microsoft stock first went on sale, it cost $21 per share. By the end of that day, the price had risen to $28 per share. Microsoft employees who had been given stock options year after year could trade their stock for cash. Or they could keep it in case the price went higher, which it did.

The stock became more and more valuable. That made some people instant millionaires—at least on paper. Two of those people were Bill Gates and Steve Ballmer. If they wanted cash, they'd have to sell some of their shares of stock. Bill sold more than $1 million worth of stock. But he still owned more Microsoft stock than any other employee. He owned 45 percent of all the shares.

Becoming a millionaire didn't change Bill much. He traveled cheaply on business trips. He drove his own car instead of hiring a limousine. He carried his own baggage at airports. And he still ordered his favorite cheeseburgers at fast-food restaurants. He did take a four-day sailing trip in Australia to celebrate the success of the stock offering. But then he returned to work with the same energy as always.

After the stock offering, Bill worried that Microsoft employees might have trouble concentrating on work. They might spend too much energy watching Microsoft's stock price on the stock market. He didn't want employees daydreaming about elaborate houses, fancy cars, or other luxuries that they might buy as their stock rose in value. Worse yet, he feared that some of his best employees might retire after becoming millionaires. Yet most employees continued to come to work every day. Bill was happy to see that hundreds of Microsoft millionaires kept working.

Playing Games

Bill's grandmother died in 1987. To honor her memory, Bill bought three and a half acres of land on the nearby Hood Canal. He built a retreat there for family gatherings. He called it Cheerio. The property included three vacation homes, tennis courts, and a spa. He also built a large structure that could be used as a business retreat. "The idea was really a tribute to [Gam], being that she was the glue that kept our family together," Mary Gates explained.

The retreat became the site of the Microgames. This festival was for friends, family, and Microsoft employees. At the Microgames, the Gates family acted as organizers and judges. The guests got to have all the fun. They were divided into teams. They solved puzzles, sang, raced, and went on treasure hunts. Each year, the games had a different theme. One year, guests found themselves on an African safari. Another year, they were in the American Wild West of the 1800s.

At the 1987 Microgames, Bill met Melinda French, a new Microsoft employee. Bill was immediately attracted to her. Melinda was smart, witty, and independent. She had grown up in Dallas, Texas, with two brothers and a sister. Her father was an aerospace engineer.

Like Bill, Melinda found math exciting. She had studied at Duke University in Durham, North Carolina. She earned her undergraduate (bachelor's) degree in computer science and engineering in only three years. (Most students earn their bachelor's degree in four years.) She then earned a master's degree from Duke's business school. There, a

Melinda French had a lot in common with Bill when they met in 1987.

Microsoft recruiting team recognized her talent. She interviewed at the Redmond offices and joined Microsoft. Upon meeting Bill at the Microgames, she and Bill began dating.

Meanwhile, Microsoft continued to make new products. In 1987, it introduced its second version of Windows and its Excel spreadsheet software. Each month, a new product support center answered more than one million calls from customers who needed help with Microsoft programs.

Microsoft had begun to work on CD-ROMs (compact discs with read-only memory). CD-ROMs looked like the next hot product. They were multimedia CDs. They could hold far more data than existing computer diskettes. In 1987, Microsoft sold its first CD-ROM, Microsoft Bookshelf. It was a single CD that held ten popular and useful reference books. When computer manufacturers made CD-ROM readers common on their new computers, Microsoft was ready.

Bill decided it was time to think about building a house for himself. In 1988 and 1989, he bought land in Medina, a city on Lake Washington. It was two miles across the lake from his parents' home. He didn't like the house that already stood on the property. So he sold it and had it hauled away by barge.

IT'S A FACT!

Real estate people found out where in Washington Bill was looking for land for his new house. They figured Bill would be willing to pay a lot of money. The price for land in this area of Washington went up by a huge amount.

Bill continued to think ahead. He knew that graphic designers and publishers would soon be working with digital images. Digital images are pictures that are scanned and stored by computers. Bill founded a company called Corbis. Corbis bought more than twenty million works of art and photography. He even bought the famous Bettmann Archive of photographs.

ABOUT CORBIS

The Corbis collection is stored in an online database. It holds pictures in many subject areas: fine arts, history, people, cultures, entertainment, science, technology, sports, and nature. For a fee, publishers can use these images in books, magazines, newspapers, or online publications. Corbis can also print posters for buyers. And it can take buyers on computerized trips around the world.

RIDING THE WAVE

**(Above)
Bill holds
the third
version of
Windows.**

ON MAY 22, 1990, Bill Gates pushed his glasses up his nose, grinned, and walked onstage at Center City in New York City. He was there to launch Windows 3.0—the third version of Windows. Thousands of reporters and computer employees watched the presentation in the audience and on television. Industry leaders praised the new Windows. A short, MTV-style video hyped the program. Microsoft ran a six-month advertising campaign. The company had spent $3 million on the launch day alone. It spent more than $10 million total to make Windows 3.0 the fastest-moving software product in the country.

Buyers snapped up more than one hundred thousand copies of Windows 3.0 in the first two weeks. By the end of 1991, Microsoft had shipped four million copies. Windows was available in twelve languages and was sold in twenty-four countries. Computer makers now included Windows as standard software on their computers. Buyers bought six million of the Microsoft mouse. Bill finally had a software best-seller.

OTHER INTERESTS

During this time, he continued to think about his dream house. He hired an architect to run an international design competition. The winner of the competition was a house to be made of concrete, steel, wood, and stone. The house would nestle into a hillside, with

IT'S A FACT!

Bill received twenty-three sets of drawing plans from around the world for his new home. He chose three finalists and met with them three times before choosing the winner.

Bill's home in Medina, Washington, was completed after several years of planning and four years of construction.

lots of windows to offer views of the lake and nearby mountains.

Investments outside of Microsoft were also on Bill's mind. As a child, he had dreamed of becoming a scientist. In October 1991, Bill gave $12 million to create the Department of Molecular Biology at the University of Washington in Seattle. The new department brought attention to the university. The school was then able to hire a famous scientist, Leroy Hood, to do research there. Hood is a leader in mapping genes in the human body. His work might lead to cures for fatal diseases. Bill had studied Hood's research on DNA and had met with him before making his donation to the university.

A few months earlier, in July 1991, Mary Gates had called her son. She said she wanted him to meet another famous person—billionaire investor Warren Buffett. Bill was very busy, but he and Melinda flew by helicopter to Cheerio. There, Buffett and other guests had already gathered. Gates and Buffett hit it off right away. They had much in common. They each had a great mind for business, a sense of humor, and a fondness for hamburgers. Buffett was impressed with Bill's business sense. "If Bill had started a hot dog stand, he would have become the hot dog king of the world," Buffett declared.

WARREN BUFFETT

Born in Nebraska in 1930, Warren Buffett began making business decisions at an early age. At the age of eleven, he'd bought his first stock— and was patient enough to wait for it to make money. He started a small investment company in the late 1950s. And by the late 1960s, he had a large and varied set of investments that was making him a rich man.

By the early 1990s, when Buffett met Bill Gates, Buffett was a billionaire and one of the world's wealthiest men. He's remained a down-to-earth person, though, and still lives in the house he bought early in his career. He gives millions of dollars to charity each year and, after his death, plans to give the rest to his foundation.

Windows 3.0 was a best-seller, but Bill didn't rest. By 1992, programmers had improved Windows in a thousand ways. Bill knew he had to keep improving the product greatly. If he didn't, no one would want to buy new versions. They would just keep using the old one. Microsoft improved Windows and its other programs. For example, the company offered its Word 2.0 word-processing program in twenty-two different languages.

Around this time, builders began digging the site for Bill's dream home. Seattle is located in an earthquake zone. So the design required tons of concrete and many beams and supports to protect the house from collapsing during an earthquake.

IT'S A FACT!

The rooms in Bill's home are programmed to play the occupants' favorite music when they enter the room.

For beams, builders recycled logs from a lumber mill that was being torn down.

Inside the house, a master computer would run the lights, temperature controls, and the security system. Flat LCDs (liquid-crystal displays) on the walls would be programmed to show different pieces of artwork.

The builders worked first on the guesthouse.
They would use it to test another new technology.
High-bandwidth wiring would allow the computers
running the house to be superfast.

LEARNING TO LOVE

Melinda French was promoted quickly at Microsoft.
She was intelligent and had good people skills. By
1993, she was a manager. She supervised the work
of about forty employees.

Bill and Melinda had dated on and off since
1987. The couple went to dinner, movies, and plays.

Bill and Melinda attend a Seattle SuperSonics basketball game in Seattle.

Once they took a trip to Australia. It became obvious to people who knew Bill well that he and Melinda had a special relationship.

Bill's parents were worried about him. He seemed to be too busy with work to have time for love. Bill's mother asked him when he was going to give Melinda an engagement ring. Finally, on March 20, 1993, Bill surprised Melinda. The couple was flying from Palm Springs, California, to Seattle. Bill had the private flight detoured to Omaha, Nebraska, Warren Buffett's hometown. There, Buffett had arranged for a famous jewelry store to be opened only for Bill and Melinda. The couple picked out a diamond engagement ring.

Two days later, Microsoft announced the engagement. The news made headlines around the world. Many people who knew Bill and Melinda thought they were well matched. "She's really a wonderful person, the perfect match for him," said Bill Gates Sr. "Very, very bright, very organized, very supportive, very interested in family and good family life."

Melinda could give Bill personal happiness. She could understand his business too, an important part of his life. Yet she was concerned

Bill and Melinda live a high-profile life. Here, they attend a party in Seattle.

about marrying the richest man in the world. She feared she would lose her privacy. She did not want to be in the newspapers. So she contacted relatives, friends, and former neighbors and teachers. She asked them not to talk about her to reporters. She was also worried about safety. Being so wealthy could make her a target for kidnappers.

Melinda wanted some changes made to Bill's dream house. After all, she was going to live there

too. She didn't like the
exposed beams and rough
concrete. She wanted her
own study and a dressing
room. She wanted a
kitchen that would suit a
family. And she wanted to
hire security guards for
protection and privacy.
She stopped working at
Microsoft and decided to
focus on working with
charities (organizations
that raised money for
people in need).

IT'S A FACT!
After her
engagement to Bill,
Melinda knew she
had to leave her job
at Microsoft. The
people Melinda
supervised had
become
uncomfortable with
her. Perhaps they
feared that their
gripes about the
company might get
back to the boss.

Bill was taking
Microsoft full speed into multimedia products. In
1993, Microsoft began to sell more CD-ROM
titles such as Microsoft Encarta. Encarta was the
first multimedia encyclopedia designed for a
computer. Encarta brought subjects to life. It had
sound, animation, illustrations, graphs, maps, and
photographs. Later, Microsoft sold other CDs.
Some focused on specific subjects, such as
dinosaurs, movies, music, baseball, and golf.

Microsoft also brought out its high-powered Windows NT (New Technology) operating system. Windows NT was made especially for businesses. With this software, businesspeople could run a whole network of computer terminals from a single PC. They could keep track of how many products they had in storage. They could keep track of sales and how much money their company earned. They could do complicated calculations. *PC Magazine* gave Windows NT an award for excellence.

5 GETTING A LIFE

BILL AND MELINDA WERE MARRIED

on January 1, 1994. The wedding was on the island of Lanai in Hawaii. They chose the island because it is privately owned. They could control who would attend the wedding. No party crashers were allowed, especially uninvited photographers. Only 130 invited guests would be there. Bill paid for the guests to stay at a hotel on the island. Bill and Melinda tried to keep the date and place of their wedding a secret, but word leaked out. The story made the newspapers. Security people turned away reporters who tried to get to the island.

On their wedding day, Melinda wore a white wedding gown. Five bridesmaids in pink gowns attended her. Bill wore a white dinner jacket and black trousers. Steve Ballmer was his best man. They exchanged vows on a cliff above the ocean. At the end of the short Roman Catholic ceremony, Bill slipped a wedding ring on Melinda's finger. "We're both extremely happy and looking forward to a long, wonderful life together," Bill later announced to the public.

Bill and Melinda had a party with their friends to celebrate their marriage the week after the ceremony.

Yet in life, joy and sorrow often mix. Shortly before the wedding, Bill learned that his mother had breast cancer. She had the best care possible. Still, the cancer overtook her within a year. In the early morning of June 10, 1994, Mary Gates died. Bill and his mother had been very close. Her death hit him hard.

Several days later, Bill spoke at his mother's memorial service. The memorial was packed with family and friends. Then Bill turned to Melinda, his family, and work to get through the difficult time.

IT'S A FACT!

When Mary Gates died, Bill got in his car and rushed to his parents' house. On the way, a police officer pulled him over for speeding. The officer recognized Bill. He saw tears streaming down Bill's face and asked what had happened. Bill explained that his mother had just died. The officer gently told Bill to drive a little slower. Then he let him go.

LIVING AS A CELEBRITY

The Federal Trade Commission (FTC) is a government agency that keeps watch over large and

successful companies. The agency's job is to make
sure companies conduct their business legally. In
1991, the FTC and the U.S. Department of Justice
(a department of the U.S. government that enforces
federal laws) began to investigate Microsoft. In
1994, Justice Department lawyers sued Microsoft
over the way the company sold its products.
Microsoft had always insisted that computer makers
who sold the Microsoft OS had to also sell other
Microsoft products. The lawsuit put an end to this
illegal practice. Even so, Bill Gates did not admit
that his company had done anything wrong.

The value of Microsoft stock continued to rise.
Bill became a billionaire. He passed Warren Buffett
at the top of the list of America's richest people. Bill
was actually not the highest-paid employee at
Microsoft. He made $525,000 a year in salary and
bonuses. But he often sold shares in the company.
He used the money from those sales to pay his
taxes, build his home, and invest in other businesses.

Bill didn't show off his wealth. He tried to keep a
low profile. But, to reporters, Bill Gates was a
celebrity. He couldn't avoid the media. But Bill
thought that talking to reporters was a waste of time.
He was impatient with what he called "stupid

questions." He earned a reputation for rudeness. Once, a television reporter asked him a mean-spirited question. The reporter said that competing with Bill was like being in a tough street fight. Bill lost his temper and walked off the stage.

He gave millions of dollars to charity. He gave computers to libraries. But people questioned these donations. They said he made them only to make his business look better. Others said he didn't give enough.

IT'S A FACT!

One Bill watcher figured out that he earned about $150 each second. At that pay rate, it wouldn't be worthwhile for Bill to pick a $500 bill off the sidewalk. He could earn more money just by walking on.

JUST FOR BILL

In 1994, Bill bought the Codex Leicester. This is an eighteen-page scientific notebook written by Leonardo da Vinci. In it, Leonardo wrote about many aspects of science. Bill had been a fan of Leonardo's since boyhood. He paid $30.8 million for the notebook. "Leonardo was one of the most amazing people who ever lived," Bill said. "I bought the manuscript for personal pleasure." When not on loan to museums, the Codex Leicester would be housed in Bill's personal library.

Bill Gates visits a school in South Dakota where the Gates Foundation paid for computers for libraries.

INVESTING IN THE FUTURE

Bill and Melinda wanted to return some of their money to society in positive ways. In 1994, they created the William H. Gates Foundation. The foundation would give money to worthy projects. Bill's father retired from his law firm to run the foundation. The foundation gave money to education, health care around the globe, arts, and other areas. Bill and Melinda also donated $1 million to the Fred Hutchinson Cancer Research

Center in Seattle. "Giving away money effectively is almost as hard as earning it in the first place," he once said.

Paul Allen had recovered from his illness. And he had stayed with Microsoft as a member of its board of directors. He and Bill wanted to do something for Lakeside School. The school had given them a chance to use a computer back when computers were rare. They wanted to say thank-you. So they paid for a new science building at Lakeside. The two friends flipped a coin to decide whose name would go first on the building. It is called Allen-Gates Hall. They named the auditorium in memory of their classmate Kent Evans, who had died in a mountain-climbing accident when the boys were in high school.

IT'S A FACT!

Bill also helped Harvard University. He and Steve Ballmer paid for a new computer center for Harvard. The price tag: $15 million from Bill, $10 million from Ballmer.

In 1994, Bill joined Craig McCaw, a pioneer in the world of cellular telephones, in an ambitious

venture. They created a company called Teledesic.
Its goal was to circle Earth with 288 low-orbiting
satellites that would provide two-way
communications for the entire world. Each of the
satellites would cost nearly $20 million to build, so
Teledesic needed many investors. "I am investing in
Teledesic because I believe it is a very exciting idea
with the potential to truly connect the world
together in a way it never has been before," Bill
said. If the satellite network succeeded, information
could travel from Earth to satellite and back at
speeds as fast as through fiber-optic cables. The
network would give people in areas without even
basic telephone service the ability to communicate
using handheld devices.

CHANGING DIRECTION

The Internet is the worldwide network of computers
linked by phone lines and cable networks. The
Internet started as a network of government
computers in the 1970s. At first, only scientists and
military officials used the Internet. Then
businesspeople discovered the system. They wanted
to use it to advertise products and services. Schools
and libraries realized that the system could be used

to spread information. More and more organizations began posting material on the Internet. This is how the World Wide Web was born.

By 1994, Bill knew that the growth of the Internet was the most important event since the creation of the personal computer. He realized that the Internet would be the communication tool of the future. Microsoft had already added hypertext markup language (HTML) to its word-processing system. HTML is used to create Web pages. He saw that he needed to make quick changes at Microsoft. Otherwise, his company would be left in the dust. Other companies were already making software for the Internet.

In 1995, Bill wrote a long e-mail to his employees. In it, he said, "Now I assign the Internet the highest level of importance. . . . Our focus on the Internet is critical to every part of our business." Bill was energized.

He wanted to add Internet tools to all Microsoft programs. Microsoft added a Web browser, Internet Explorer, to the newest Windows OS. The browser let PC users bring Internet sites to their own computer screens. Microsoft made software for networks of computers that could work

The monitor in the background shows a later version of Microsoft's Web browser, Internet Explorer.

together over the Internet. Microsoft also made software for creating websites with graphics, animation, video, and audio. It also made software for companies that put websites on the Internet. Bill described the new focus: "All of our products treat the Internet as the big opportunity," he said.

Meanwhile, Bill and Melinda made a special gift to honor Bill's mother, Mary. On the anniversary of her death, they donated $10 million to the University of Washington. The money established the Mary Gates Endowment for Students. Mary had always placed a high value on education. With this scholarship (money to be used for education), many undergraduate students would benefit.

WINDOWS 95

In mid-1995, Microsoft launched Windows 95. It was a new operating system—and a whole lot more. Its overall design was simple and clean. It made complicated jobs easy to do. On August 24, 1995, fifteen large white tents decorated the lawn outside Microsoft headquarters. It felt like a circus. Bill Gates and Jay Leno, host of *The Tonight Show*, were in one tent. People from other software companies were in the fourteen other tents. They showed off programs designed to run on Windows 95.

Bill came onstage with Leno. Bill wore white slacks and a navy blue sport shirt with the Windows logo. He and Leno traded jokes. Bill remarked, "Windows 95 is so easy, even a talk show host can figure it out." Then Leno introduced Windows 95 to the twenty-five thousand specially invited guests.

Microsoft also launched its own online service, Microsoft Network (MSN). It was like other online services. People could pay Microsoft a fee each month

for Internet connection. Then they could use Internet features like e-mail, news services, banking services, and chat rooms. Windows 95 sold rapidly. But not many users joined the new online network. Microsoft tried again. Within a year, it had redesigned MSN. People began to join the network. Still, not enough people joined to give Microsoft a profit.

After launching Windows 95, Bill took time off to travel. He and Melinda took a two-week trip to China. A group of friends joined them, including Bill Gates Sr. and Warren Buffett.

CHINESE TERRA-COTTA WARRIORS

While in China, Bill bought a full-size copy of an ancient Chinese statue. More than two thousand years ago, after his death, a Chinese emperor had himself buried in a massive tomb. Inside the tomb were eight thousand life-sized warriors made out of a type of pottery called terra-cotta. Each statue was individually carved. Each face was different from the others. Alongside the warriors were chariots and weapons. The battle-ready warriors were to show how powerful the emperor was during his rule. The tomb was discovered in 1974 and has yet to be fully explored.

They traveled by train and boat through the country. At the Great Wall of China (an ancient wall that winds across four thousand miles in China), Bill tried to fly a kite. But the wind wouldn't cooperate. After viewing the scenery and sightseeing, Bill played bridge. Melinda also organized fun activities, like karaoke singing (singing the words of popular songs while a machine plays the music) and trivia quizzes.

The Gateses and their friends visited the capital city of Beijing. There, Bill met with Chinese leader and Communist Party president Jiang Zemin. Bill, Melinda, and Warren Buffett posed for photos with Jiang. Bill also paid a quick visit to Microsoft's

Beijing office. And he bought a nine-foot-tall clay statue of a Chinese warrior. It was a copy of a famous statue that had been unearthed by scientists.

BACK AT HOME

Bill and Melinda's new home was almost completed. He and Melinda decided it was close enough to have a party there for his fortieth birthday. Bill had taken up golf. For the party, Melinda had an eighteen-hole miniature golf course set up on the grounds. She and Bill dressed in old-fashioned golfing clothes. The eighty guests came in costume too. Melinda invited four of Bill's female friends to come dressed as cheerleaders. Their lettered sweaters spelled out B-I-L-L.

Bill was ready to get back to work. He wanted to teach people about computers and Microsoft. He began writing a newspaper column. It was published by the *New York Times* and on Microsoft's website. In some columns, he answered readers' questions. He explained how small businesses might use computers. He told young people what they should study if they wanted a job working with computers. And he talked about which future technologies might become important. In other columns, Bill wrote about the qualities that make someone a good manager, employee, or computer programmer. Readers could send questions directly to Bill by e-mail at askbill@microsoft.com.

THINKING ABOUT THE FUTURE

In November 1995, Bill published the first edition of *The Road Ahead.* In this book, he described the history of computing and predicted future trends. A year later, he published a revised edition of the book. This edition focused more on the Internet. Both books were best-sellers in more than twenty countries. Bill earned $3 million from the sale of *The Road Ahead.* He gave that money to the National Foundation for the Improvement of Education. This is a nonprofit organization. It helps teachers learn to use computers and other technology in their classrooms.

Bill explains in *The Road Ahead* that he has always tried to take the long view. That means he looks far into the future and plans ahead. He tries to make choices that will be good for his company over a long period, not just in the near future. But technology changes very quickly. It is difficult to know what will happen in the future.

Personal computers were first made thirty years ago. Since then, they have been getting more and more powerful. They have more memory and can work faster. In *The Road Ahead*, Bill says that faster, more powerful computers will lead to more products.

CHAPTER 6

HAVING IT ALL

(Above) Bill and Melinda go to many charity functions together.

BILL GATES HAD COME FAR since 1975, when he left Harvard to follow his dream. He had started a successful company from scratch. He had become very rich. He had married the love of his life. What was left for him to do?

When he was younger, Bill hadn't wanted a family. He hadn't wanted to settle down. He

even said that children scared him. But then
Melinda came on the scene. And then he became
"Uncle Trey" to his sister's children. Bill's views
slowly changed.

On April 26, 1996, Melinda gave birth to a
daughter, Jennifer Katharine Gates. Bill was at her
side for the birth. Later, he joked that more than
just business worries kept
him up at night. The baby
kept him up too. He kept
a photograph at work of
himself holding Jennifer.
Bill's father was happy to
see his son in this new
role. "He just loves that
little girl," said Bill Gates
Sr. "It's so marvelous to
see. . . . It's really
gratifying."

IT'S A FACT!

Bill once sang
"Twinkle Twinkle
Little Star" for
Barbara Walters
while being
interviewed for the
TV show *20/20*. She
had asked him what
Jennifer's favorite
lullaby was.

On the business front,
MSNBC came out in July 1996. MSNBC was a
joint project between Microsoft and the NBC
television network. The project brought news and
information to television viewers through the
MSNBC channel. Internet users could get even

The MSNBC newsroom

more information on the MSNBC website, www.msnbc.com. They could also read an online magazine called *Slate*.

COMING HOME

Construction on Bill's house had dragged on for six years. Bill thought that neighbors might be tired of the construction vehicles, noise, and dust. So he hired work crews to do things for his neighbors. The crews mowed neighbors' lawns, washed the dust off their vehicles, and other tasks.

By late 1997, the house still wasn't quite done. But the Gates family moved in anyway. The home is made up of five buildings connected by

underground tunnels. One building holds a grand
entry hall, guestrooms, and a dining room that seats
120 people. It also has a theater, meeting rooms, a
computer room, and a library. Another building
contains a beach house, hot tub, and swimming
pool. Another holds a caretaker's home. The
family's private living space takes up two floors of
the main building. It includes a family room, an
exercise room, a trampoline room, and bedrooms.
Parking space for twenty
cars is hidden
underground. There, Bill
keeps his collection of
sports cars. The land
includes wetlands and a
trout stream.

Bill had waited seven
years and paid more than
$54 million for his house.
So he expected everything
to work. Yet he wrote in
his newspaper column
about one problem. He
had a movable television screen set up at the end of
his bed. One night, the screen wouldn't move down

It's a Fact!

The library is Bill's
favorite room. He
hired a book dealer
to help choose the
books. "It all goes
back to the early
experience that both
Melinda and I had
growing up with
libraries in our
communities," he
explained.

when he was done watching. It wouldn't even turn
off. Instead, it glowed bright blue. Bill had to throw
a blanket over it so he could go to sleep.

Bill and Melinda continued to donate money to
charities. They gave $100 million to a health
organization. The organization gives medicine to
children in poor countries to protect them against
disease. In June of 1997, they created the Gates
Library Foundation (www.glf.org). They gave $200
million to the foundation. Its purpose is to provide
computers and Internet access to public libraries in
low-income areas of the United States and Canada.
With the Internet, someone in a poor area can use the
same resources as those in wealthier neighborhoods,
Bill pointed out.

Bill tried to downplay his wealth. But being rich
did cause some problems. In March 1997, Bill
received a frightening letter. The writer was a young
man named Adam Quinn Pletcher. He threatened to
kill Gates if he didn't pay him $5 million. Federal
Bureau of Investigation (FBI) agents caught the man.
He was also wanted for cheating people out of money
on the Internet. When Pletcher went on trial, Bill was
in Belgium for business. On his way to meet with
Belgian officials, Bill got a surprise. Pranksters shoved

two custard pies in his face. He was surprised but
unhurt. He just wiped his face and glasses and went
on to the meeting. He later joked, "The worst part
was that the pies were not very tasty."

TESTIFYING BEFORE CONGRESS

On March 2, 1998, Bill met Melinda in
Washington, D.C. Like other tourists, they visited
the Capitol and the National Gallery. They grabbed
a quick pizza for dinner. Then they went back to
their hotel. Bill wanted to prepare for the next day.
He and other computer company leaders would
testify about the computer business before members
of the U.S. Congress. He finished typing up notes
on his laptop computer. He practiced his five-
minute speech.

Bill told the members of Congress how
Microsoft had succeeded. The company had earned
its success by always improving its products. He
said that many computer software makers were
offering products for sale. This competition among
many companies kept software prices low. He said
that the government should not interfere in the
computer business by telling software makers how
to design their products. Other computer company

Bill Gates

Bill testifies before the Senate Judiciary Committee.

leaders spoke at the hearing too. After the hearing, Bill signed autographs and talked with reporters.

Then Bill and Melinda flew to New York City. Bill had been invited to a fancy dinner at Radio City Music Hall. The event was to celebrate the seventy-fifth anniversary of *Time* magazine. At this dinner, famous guests gave short speeches. They talked about important people of the twentieth century. Bill was asked to speak about the Wright brothers, inventors of the airplane. He was a little nervous. He was used to speaking to computer specialists, not to celebrities. All the same, his speech went well.

The next morning, Bill visited a school in New York's Harlem area, where many African Americans live. There, he spoke with a group of sixth graders. These students were using laptop computers to improve their learning skills. Then he visited the New York Public Library. There, he talked with TV reporter Charlie Rose.

Finally, the busy week ended. Bill was glad to get home to see Jennifer. She was now two years old. She and "Dada" liked to play together and read books. They played with a Barney program on the computer that features the lovable purple dinosaur. Bill had to be careful not to say the word *computer* around Jennifer. If he did, she would follow him around, saying "'puter, 'puter, 'puter," until he played the game with her. "I'm very lucky. My daughter is a very happy, joyful person," Bill said.

In July, Bill threw a party at Microsoft headquarters. The party was to celebrate the launch of Windows 98. Until then, Windows programs had been made especially for business PC users.

Windows 98 was the first OS made especially with home PC users in mind.

BATTLING IN THE COURTS

In 1998, Bill announced a new president for his Microsoft Corporation. Steve Ballmer would be in charge of the daily work of Microsoft. That way, Bill could return to his first love–creating new products. Bill would work with different teams in the company. He would create software and computer services.

Steve Ballmer became president of Microsoft in 1998.

"Microsoft is almost a quarter-century old, but we are just at the beginning," Bill wrote. "The future makes me very excited. . . . We can all be . . . proud of what we've built so far. But the future [will be better than] everything we've achieved to date."

But nobody knew for sure what the future would be for Microsoft. Legal battles were likely to come. The owners of some computer companies said Microsoft was a monopoly. A monopoly is a company that has nearly complete control of an industry. A monopoly can control the prices of the products it sells. It can charge unfairly high prices. Or it can sell products at very low prices that other companies cannot match. Buyers prefer the lower prices, so the companies with higher prices risk going out of business. Nine out of ten new computers sold in 1998 had Microsoft's Windows 95 already on them. Some people thought that gave the company a monopoly on personal computer operating systems. It's not against the law for a company to be a monopoly, but it is illegal if the monopoly harms consumers.

In October 1998, the U.S. Justice Department and eighteen states sued Microsoft. At the trial, government lawyers tried to prove that Microsoft held a monopoly on operating systems. They also tried to prove that this monopoly harmed consumers. Also, they said Microsoft acted illegally to keep other makers of Internet browsers from competing.

Bill Gates did not speak at the trial. But government lawyers had already asked him questions on videotape. They showed parts of the videotape on a large screen during the trial. Reporters wrote stories guessing what would happen at the end of the trial. They wondered what the trial would mean for Microsoft and Bill.

The trial moved at a fast pace. In December, the attorney general of South Carolina decided the case against Microsoft was weak and removed his state from the trial. After a two-week holiday recess, the trial resumed in January 1999.

Next, Microsoft lawyers made their case. They called witnesses who said that Microsoft did not harm consumers. The witnesses said that Microsoft offered computer users improved products at good prices. They also talked about the tough competition Microsoft faced.

In March, Judge Thomas Penfield Jackson, the judge presiding over the case, ordered a three-month recess so that he could try another case. During the break, government lawyers talked with Microsoft lawyers. But the two sides could not come to an out-of-court agreement. The trial started up again in June of 1999. The final witness left the stand on the seventy-sixth day of the trial. Finally, the trial was over. The judge had a lot of information and testimony to think about. Then he would announce his verdict, or decision.

BUSINESS @ THE SPEED OF THOUGHT

What was Gates doing while the trial went on? He continued his daily work at Microsoft. Also, he finished his new book, *Business @ the Speed of Thought.* Gates thought that business operations would change a great deal over the next ten years. Computers make more information available to workers. So the workers need to learn how to use this information to improve their companies. In his book, Gates suggested ways for

IT'S A FACT!

Business @ the Speed of Thought came out in March of 1999. Gates gave interviews and went on television shows to help sell it. Again, he gave much of the money from the sales of the book to charity.

business leaders to use digital information. He gave examples of how some companies were doing so already.

Also in March, Microsoft launched Internet Explorer 5.0. This was an improved version of the company's Web browser. Within a week, users had downloaded a million copies of the browser from the Internet.

Bill and Melinda were also awaiting the birth of their second child. Rory John Gates was born on May 23, 1999. Bill took a short leave from Microsoft.

MICROSOFT MONOPOLY

In November 1999, Judge Jackson ruled on the Microsoft case. He said that Microsoft was a monopoly. It had a monopoly in two areas. One was on OSs, and the other was on Web browsers. Jackson said that these monopolies hurt consumers.

The judge talked about several examples of Microsoft's attempts to hurt other companies. One example was Intel, a maker of computer chips. In 1995, Intel was working on a product that Microsoft thought would cut into sales of

Windows. Bill met with Intel's chief executive officer (CEO, the manager in charge of running a company) many times. He said Intel had to stop developing their new product. If they didn't, Microsoft would not make products that worked with PCs run by Intel chips. Intel needed Microsoft's products to work with their chips. So they stopped developing the product. Later, Bill wrote an e-mail to other Microsoft bosses. He said, "If Intel is not sticking totally to its part of the deal let me know." There were other examples. Judge Jackson said that these examples showed "the pressure that Microsoft is willing to apply" to companies that don't want to cooperate.

Bill Gates said that the ruling was only one small step in a long process. He planned to fight the ruling. In December 1999, Microsoft bosses met with the Department of Justice lawyers. They tried to settle on a solution. But the two sides could not agree on what should be done. It was up to Judge Jackson to decide how to fix the monopoly. He ordered Microsoft to be broken up into two separate companies.

The Microsoft team appealed. That means they asked a higher court to look at the case. The

Judge Thomas Jackson believed Microsoft held a monopoly.

appeals court had seven judges. Maybe they would come to a different decision. They did. In June 2001, the appeals court ruled. It upheld part of Judge Jackson's decision. It said that Microsoft did have a monopoly on OSs. But it also changed part of the original decision. It said that Microsoft did not have a monopoly on Web browsers.

That fall, a federal judge ordered Microsoft and the Department of Justice and the eighteen states to settle on a way to fix the monopoly. Later that year, Microsoft, the Department of Justice, and nine of the states agreed on a fix. Microsoft would have to share some of its computer code with other companies. And it would not be allowed to charge unfair prices for its products. Prices that were very low kept other companies from competing. Federal (U.S.) employees would keep watch on Microsoft to make sure they followed the rules.

Many people thought this fix would not be good enough. They said that Microsoft would still have a monopoly. They wanted Microsoft to be broken up into smaller companies. Some of the people who thought so were lawyers for nine of the states that were suing Microsoft. But the judge approved the fix that Microsoft, the Department of Justice, and the other nine states had agreed on. After a while, most of the remaining states agreed to it. The only state not to was Massachusetts. It appealed the decision and asked for a harsher punishment for Microsoft. But in July 2004, the state's appeal was denied.

BILL AND SPORTS CARS

Bill loves fast cars. Over the years, he has gotten many speeding tickets. In high school, he owned an orange red Mustang convertible. In the early days of Microsoft, Bill bought himself a Porsche 930 Turbo. He later added a Lexus and a Ferrari 348. Several more Porsches followed, including a Porsche 959 valued at about one million dollars.

In 1997, Bill and his close friend, Andy Evans, invested in Professional SportsCar Racing, Inc. (PSR). They bought two racetracks and tried to bring international teams into the U.S.-led sport. The industry responded by creating its own rival sports car racing program. By December of 1997, PSR had been sold. But many people wondered what Bill has in store for the world of sports car racing.

The first Porsche that Bill bought was a 930 like the one above.

MICROSOFT VS. EUROPE

Finally, Microsoft's monopoly problems in the United States were over. But Microsoft had also been sued by the European Commission (EC, a branch of government of the European Union, a grouping of European nations) for being a monopoly harmful to consumers. The EC said Microsoft was a monopoly because of its strategy (plan) of bundling, or including other pieces of software along with Windows. It said that bundling limited the choices that consumers had.

The EC focused its case on the media player that Microsoft included with every copy of Windows it sold. The media player was software that played music and movies on a computer. The commission said that including the media player with Windows limited the choice consumers had to use other media players. In December of 2004, a European court ordered Microsoft to offer a version of Windows without its media player software. Microsoft was also ordered to pay a fine of $655.5 million.

The ruling on software bundling applied only to Europe. But it was important because it was the first time Microsoft had been ordered to stop bundling its software products and features with

Windows. Bundling is one of Microsoft's most basic and important marketing strategies. Still,

IT'S A FACT!

Bundling has become a standard marketing plan because of Microsoft.

Microsoft only had to offer a version of Windows without the media player. It could still offer a version of Windows that *did* bundle the media player. In January of 2005, it announced it would do what the court ordered–but it planned to appeal the decision in a higher court.

CHAPTER 7

ROCKING THROUGH THE DAY

BILL GATES NO LONGER SPENDS
sixteen hours a day at his office. He no
longer stays up two nights in a row and
crashes on his office floor for a nap. After
getting married, the boss cut his workday to
twelve hours each day during the week. On
weekends, he works eight hours each day. He
even takes off some weekends to play golf or

(Above)
Although his
company
keeps Bill
busy, he
does take
time out for
golfing and
other
activities.

take vacations with his family. And he's still adding to his growing family. Bill and Melinda's third child, Phoebe Adele Gates, was born in 2002.

Other software makers hoped that married life would distract Bill from his work at Microsoft. Yet Bill still works hard. And he doesn't like to waste a minute. He has a personal assistant and uses an online calendar to manage his time. He also often reviews how he is spending his time. He wants to see if and how he could use it more wisely.

He has a short drive from his home on Lake Washington to the Microsoft campus in Redmond. From the outside, Microsoft world headquarters looks more like a college than a business center. Its twenty-five redbrick buildings are lined with windows that give a view of the lawns.

BILL'S DAY

On the inside, Bill works in an office much like everyone else's. It has a desk with a chair, a sofa, and a coffee table. Bill works from two computers at the same time. He runs the company mostly by e-mail. Every day, he gets hundreds of e-mails from Microsoft employees worldwide. He spends hours each day sending out e-mails of his own. Each month, he meets with his top managers. They go over business strategy.

Lake Bill 2 on Microsoft's Redmond, Washington, campus

Microsoft has a company library. Bill uses it a lot. He reads the *Wall Street Journal*, the *Sunday New York Times*, the *Economist*, and weekly news magazines. And, of course, he gets information from the Internet. If anything, Bill wishes he had more time each day to read.

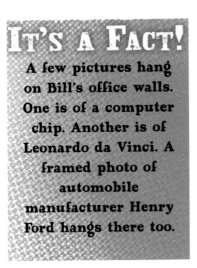

IT'S A FACT!
A few pictures hang on Bill's office walls. One is of a computer chip. Another is of Leonardo da Vinci. A framed photo of automobile manufacturer Henry Ford hangs there too.

What does Bill do all day? He does not work directly on software. Instead, he reviews the programmers' work. He asks questions and gives feedback about products. Sometimes talks can get pretty intense. When they do, Bill rocks to and fro. The rocking is one of Bill's trademarks. He says the motion still helps him think.

Bill will say so if he thinks an idea is a waste of time. He is famous for the phrase, "That's the dumbest idea I have ever heard." But he is talking only about the idea—not the person presenting it. Bill wrote his first software program, for tic-tac-toe, nearly forty years ago.

Still, Bill is excited about the process. He loves being with smart and creative people. Making new products is still fun.

How can writing software be both art and science? Everyone knows that programmers must have good math and thinking skills. That's the science part. But how will the program look on screen? How will it feel? This part of the job means software designers must have a sense of style. And even math can be artistic. Lines of computer code that do a job in the best way are beautiful in Bill's eyes.

CARING ABOUT EMPLOYEES

Bill likes creativity and hard work. He leads his company by example. Some evenings he wanders around the company buildings. He peeks in offices to see who is around. He looks at pictures that workers have put on their office walls. He tries to get a sense of how people feel about their work. He might ask one of the workers for opinions about company projects or technology.

Bill believes that the employees are the core of Microsoft. Without them, Microsoft could never get products out. The company rewards employees for their creativity and hard work. It gives them good salaries, promotions, and valuable Microsoft stock.

Bill tries to hire smart and creative people. He insists that the company hire college graduates, even though Bill dropped out of college. Microsoft sends people to colleges all over the country. Their job is to find the brightest programmers and businesspeople available.

Bill spends about three months of each year traveling. On these trips, each workday might last sixteen hours. When he arrives somewhere, he meets with Microsoft's local representatives. He also talks about Microsoft products to audiences of all kinds: government officials, business leaders, students, and the press. Also, he listens to computer users.

Every year, Bill and other top employees take a weeklong retreat from the office. Bill calls this time "Think Week." And that's what they do. They do research, think, and talk about the future. They set priorities for Microsoft. The company is working on a new version of Windows, which it plans to release in 2006. It is code-named Longhorn, and will be easier to use than previous versions of Windows and more secure.

Bill smiles during a convention in Michigan in April 2005.

At some point, Bill plans to hire someone else to run Microsoft. Until then, he'll continue to work. "I work hard because I love my work," Bill explains. "I often say I have the best job in the world, and I mean it."

Bill and Microsoft have faced problems over the years. But no matter what, he and his company have continued to do well. Few people would deny Bill's importance to the computer world. He has helped create huge changes in technology. His donations to charities are also making a big difference in the world. Some day, people who study history will look back on Bill's times. When they do, they will think of him as one of the world's most important people.

bug: a flaw in a computer program

CD-ROM: a compact disc with read-only memory; a compact disc containing graphics, sound, text, or other data that can be read by a computer

chip: an integrated circuit; a tiny piece of silicon holding the network of electronic components (parts) that form the "brains" of a computer

code: a set of instructions for a computer

digital: describing a computer or other item in which information is stored as numbers

download: to transfer data from a computer or the Internet to another computer

graphical user interface (GUI): a computer program that allows a user to interact easily with the computer, typically by using a mouse to make choices from menus or groups of icons

hardware: the physical parts of a computer

hypertext markup language (HTML): a computer language used to create Web pages

icon: a graphic symbol on a computer screen that represents an application, file, or command

language: a system of computer communication with specific rules and vocabulary

mainframe computer: a large, powerful computer used by a business or institution to perform many tasks

online: connected to or available through a computer network

operating system: software that controls the main operations of a computer and directs the processing of programs

program: coded instructions for running a specific computer operation

software: the programs and procedures of a computer system

spreadsheet: an accounting program for a computer

Teletype: a machine used to communicate, via telephone lines, with a mainframe computer

What You See Is What You Get (WYSIWYG): a computer display that exactly reflects the printed document

word processing: creating and editing documents on a computer

SOURCE NOTES

6 Bill Gates, *The Road Ahead*, (New York: Viking, 1995), 172.

9 Stephen Manes and Paul Andrews, *Gates* (New York: Doubleday, 1993), 24.

10 Walter Isaacson, "In Search of the Real Bill Gates," *Time*, January 13, 1997.

14 Gates, *The Road Ahead*, 1.

15 Isaacson, 48.

15 Gates, *The Road Ahead*, 18.

16 Ibid.

18 Ibid.

20 Ibid., 290–91

23 Isaacson, 48.

55 Alan Deutschman, "Bill Gates' Next Challenge," *Fortune*, December 28, 1992.

58 *Bill Gates*, VHS (Arts and Entertainment Network, Biography Series: 1998).

63 David Ellis, "Love Bytes: Computer Whiz Bill Gates Ends His Reign as America's Richest Bachelor," *People Weekly*, January 17, 1994.

66 Bill Gates, "Ask Bill," *http://www.microsoft.com* (January 17, 1995).

68 "The William H. Gates Foundation," *http://www.microsoft.com*. (September 3, 1998).

69 Gates, "The Future of Communications." n. d., *http://www.microsoft.com*.

70 Michael J. Miller, "Interview: Bill Gates, Microsoft," *PC Magazine*, March 25, 1997, 233.

71 Brent Schlender, "Whose Internet Is It Anyway?" *Fortune*, December 11, 1995, 126.

72 Ibid.

79 *Bill Gates*, VHS, Arts and Entertainment Network.

81 Leonard Kniffel, "Gates Expands Access Mission during Alabama Visit," *American Libraries*, April 1, 1998.

83 Jean Seligmann, "Now, an Antitrust Violation?" *Newsweek*, February 16, 1998, 64.

85 "Chairman Gates, Up Close and Personal," *U.S. News and World Report*, October 19, 1998, 15.

87 Bill Gates, "Bill Gates's Memo to Employees," news release, *http://www.microsoft.com* (September 3, 1998).

91 Brent Schlender, "On the Road with Chairman Bill," *Fortune*, May 26, 1997.

91 Judge Thomas P. Jackson, "Microsoft Antitrust Trial Findings of Fact," *http://www.news.findlaw.com/microsoft.html*. (January 5, 2000).

103 Michael J. Martinez, "New Roles Seem to Be a Natural Fit for Microsoft's Leaders," *Associated Press*, January 14, 2000.

SELECTED BIBLIOGRAPHY

BOOKS

Gates, Bill. *The Road Ahead.* New York: Viking, 1995.

Lowe, Janet. *Bill Gates Speaks.* New York: John Wiley and Sons, 1998.

Manes, Stephen, and Paul Andrews. *Gates: How Microsoft's Mogul Reinvented an Industry—and Made Himself the Richest Man in America.* New York: Doubleday, 1993.

Wallace, James. *Overdrive: Bill Gates and the Race to Control Cyberspace.* New York: John Wiley and Sons, 1997.

Wallace, James, and Jim Erickson. *Hard Drive: Bill Gates and the Making of the Microsoft Empire.* New York: John Wiley and Sons, 1992.

MAGAZINE ARTICLES

Isaacson, Walter. "In Search of the Real Bill Gates." *Time,* January 13, 1997, 44–56.

Miller, Michael J. "Interview: Bill Gates, Microsoft." *PC Magazine,* March 25, 1997, 230–34.

Schlender, Brent. "What Bill Gates Really Wants." *Fortune,* January 16, 1995, 34–47.

NEWSPAPER ARTICLES

Carlson, Caron. "Antitrust Decision Is Upheld; a Federal Appeals Court Denied the Last Challenge to the Antitrust Settlement Microsoft Corp." *eWeek,* July 5, 2004.

Elhauge, Einer. "Competition Wins in Court." *New York Times,* June 30, 2001.

Labaton, Stephen, and Steve Lohr. "Justice Department and Microsoft Are Seen in Tentative Settlement." *New York Times,* November 1, 2001.

Lohr, Steve. "For Microsoft, a Season of Triumph." *New York Times,* December 17, 2001.

Lohr, Steve, and Paul Meller. "Europe Rejects Microsoft's Bid to Preserve Bundling Plan." *New York Times,* December 23, 2004.

"Microsoft's Illegal Monopoly." *New York Times,* April 4, 2000.

Vise, David A. "Microsoft Acts on Antitrust Ruling; Windows without Media Player Will Be Available in Europe." *Washington Post,* January 25, 2005.

ONLINE PUBLICATIONS

Bill and Melinda Gates Foundation. http://www.glf.org (June 2005).

Microsoft Museum. http://www.microsoft.com/museum/default.mspx (June 2005).

"What Is Windows 'Longhorn'?" *Microsoft.com.* http://www.microsoft.com/windows/longhorn/default.mspx (June 2005).

FURTHER READING AND WEBSITES

Bill & Melinda Gates Foundation
http://www.gatesfoundation.org
The official foundation site includes articles about current national and international issues, the history of the foundation, information about seeking grants, and also a description of past grants given to other programs and organizations.

Bill Gates' Website
http://www.microsoft.com/billgates
Part of the Microsoft website, this Web page contains a brief biography on Bill Gates as well as links to his speeches and published writings.

Boyd, Aaron. *Smart Money: The Story of Bill Gates,* rev. ed. Greensboro, NC: Morgan Reynolds Publishing, 2004.

Collier, Bruce. *Charles Babbage and the Engines of Perfection.* New York: Oxford University Press, 1998.

Dickinson, Joan D. *Bill Gates: Billionaire Computer Genius.* Springfield, NJ: Enslow Publishers, 1997.

Lowe, Janet. *Bill Gates Speaks: Insight from the World's Greatest Entrepreneur.* New York: John Wiley & Sons, Inc., 1998.

Northrup, Mary. *American Computer Pioneers.* Springfield, NJ: Enslow Publishers, 1998.

Peters, Craig. *Bill Gates: Software Genius of Microsoft.* Berkeley Heights, NJ: Enslow Publishers, 2003.

Raatma, Lucia. *Bill Gates: Computer Programmer and Entrepreneur.* Chicago: Ferguson Publishing Company, 2000.

Sherman, Josepha. *Bill Gates: Computer King.* Brookfield, CT: Millbrook Press, 2000.

Sherman, Josepha. *The History of the Personal Computer.* New York: Franklin Watts, 2003.

Simon, Charnan. *Bill Gates: Helping People Use Computers.* New York: Children's Press, 1997.

Williams, Brian. *Computers.* Chicago: Heinemann Library, 2002.

Woog, Adam. *Bill Gates.* San Diego: Lucent Books, 1999.

Wukovits, John F. *Bill Gates: Software King.* New York: Franklin Watts, 2000.

INDEX

PHOTO ACKNOWLEDGMENTS

The images in this book are used with permission of: © Dan Herrick-KPA/ZUMA Press, p. 4; Classmates.com Yearbook Archives, p. 10; © Courtesy of Microsoft Corp., pp. 13, 25, 27, 37, 44, 80, 86, 99; © Doug Wilson/CORBIS, pp. 29, 30; © Starz Behind Barz/ZUMA Press, p. 33; © Roger Ressmeyer/CORBIS, p. 42; © AP/Wide World Photos, pp. 49, 63; © Ralf-Finn Hestoft/CORBIS, p. 52; © Reuters/CORBIS, pp. 54, 67; © SIEGEL MIKE/SEATTLES TIMES/CORBIS SYGMA, p. 57; © Getty Images, pp. 59, 78, 97; © Reuters, p. 71; © Time Life Pictures/Getty Images, p. 73; © AFP/Getty Images, p. 84; © RAAB SHANNA/CORBIS SYGMA, p. 92; © Artemis Images, p. 94; © REBECCA COOK/Reuters/Corbis, p. 103.

Cover image: © Courtesy of Microsoft Corp.